MW00567534

BROKEN BRANCHES

HAS THE CHURCH
REPLACED
ISRAEL?

Zola Levitt is a Jewish believer thoroughly educated in the synagogues and brought to the Messiah in 1971. He holds degrees from Duquesne University, Indiana University and an honorary Th.D. from Faith Bible College. He has, in his Christian walk, addressed millions of people concerning the facts of the Bible through his national television program, *Zola Levitt Presents*, which is carried on the major Christian networks, FAM (or CBN), FAM NET, TBN and INSP, and numerous large city broadcast stations.

Zola Levitt Ministries, Inc. is a teaching and evangelistic association guided by the standard of Romans 1:16, "To the Jew first, and also to the Gentile." Like the Apostle Paul, we work through the Gentiles to reach the Jews. We inform our Gentile viewers and listeners of those principles of the faith which will be most helpful to them in understanding and witnessing to their Jewish friends. Our ministry offers a wide variety of teaching materials including books, cassette tapes, music, video tapes, and some imported gift items from the Holy Land. A current list of these materials is available at no charge by writing to: ZOLA, Box 12268, Dallas, TX 75225.

Broken Branches
Has the Church Replaced Israel?

If some of the branches have been broken off, and you, though a wild olive shoot, have been grafted in among the others and now share in the nourishing sap from the olive root, do not boast over those branches. If you do, consider this: You do not support the root, but the root supports you. -- Romans 11:17-18 (NIV)

Our subject is replacement theology, a doctrine that has been around almost as long as the church has been in existence. Its adherents say that since Israel was "broken off" because of its rejection of the Messiah, it has been replaced by the church. All of God's promises to Israel from the Old Testament, including God's covenant with Abraham, would then apply to the church rather than to Abraham's descendants.

Have the Jews as the Chosen People, the nation of Israel fathered by Abraham, been replaced by the church? Does it no longer have any part in God's plan? If the Jews have lost their unique place in God's plan as descendants of Abraham, can a Jew become a Christian and still be a Jew, or would he then be a Gentile? Replacement theology has led to much confusion on these and other issues.

In reality, the church is an organization of both Jews and Gentiles who believe in Jesus Christ, today as it always was. It may seem to onlookers that Gentile Christians have utterly taken over the faith in the Jewish Messiah, but as Paul points out in Romans 11, there has always been a remnant of Jews in the church. Replacement theologians make the error of seeing the church as different than it is. They seem to regard it as a result of the salvation of Gentiles and divorced from its original Jewish heritage. But the salvation of the Gentiles in the first place was a Jewish mission. Jews were the first Christians and they carried their blessing to the Gentiles among them, as was the will of God.

The church seems entirely Gentile, because after all, every church is just packed with Gentiles. But if we examine the Bible and the birth of the church, a very different picture emerges than the one painted by replacement theologians.

I want to start with the whole issue of Gentile salvation, beginning with its history. It did not start in the same way as the salvation of the Jews. During His work on earth, the Lord witnessed to a handful of Gentiles and a few were saved. The people of the town of the Samaritan woman certainly were saved (John 4), as well as the Phoenician woman whose daughter was vexed with a devil (Matthew 15) and the Roman officer whose servant was healed by the Lord (Matthew 8). But other than the few extraordinary cases, the Lord's ministry was to the Jews. In fact, He instructed His disciples as follows:

> *Go not into the way of the Gentiles, and into any city of the Samaritans enter ye not: but go rather to the lost sheep of the house of Israel. -- Matthew 10:5-6*

On the whole, Gentile salvation waited until the book of Acts and the career of Peter, who was really the Apostle to the Jews. He had preached the sermon at Pentecost in Acts 2, where

3,000 Jews were saved, and with John healed the lame man at the Temple gate (Acts 3:1 - 4:4), winning another 5,000 souls.

But on one significant occasion, Peter was called to a Gentile household. I refer to Acts 10, where it says:

> *There was a certain man in Caesarea called Cornelius, a centurion of the band called the Italian band. . . . -- vs. 1*

Cornelius was an officer in the Roman army, and yet he was a devout man, as stated in verse 2:

> *A devout man, and one that feared God with all his house, which gave much alms to the people, and prayed to God alway.*

He may have been one of the halfway converts to Judaism, those people who did not undertake mikvah (ritual bathing) and circumcision, but who did follow certain Jewish practices. They came to the worship services and watched what went on, and they admired Judaism and did not worship the Roman gods, who had all too human attributes and foibles. They went to the real God of Judaism, which took them in the direction of the real Messiah. Cornelius had a dream to send for Peter, and that Apostle, the great fisherman, came to his house.

> *And as he talked with him, he went in, and found many that were come together. And he said unto them, Ye know how that it is an unlawful thing for a man that is a Jew to keep company, or come unto one of another nation; but God hath showed me that I should not call*

any man common or unclean. -- vss. 27-28

According to ancient Jewish law, Peter should not have frater-nized with Gentiles so closely as to visit in their homes, eat with them, and so forth. Yet here he was, associating with them. He said:

Therefore came I unto you without gainsaying, as soon as I was sent for: I ask therefore for what intent ye have sent for me? -- vs. 29

Cornelius then described his dream and the specific instruc-tions he was given to send for Peter.

Then Peter opened his mouth, and said, Of a truth I perceive that God is no respecter of persons: But in every nation he that feareth him, and worketh righteous-ness, is accepted with him. -- vss. 34-35

"God is no respecter of persons" has often been used by Cau-casians to allow non-whites to come into the church -- blacks, Hispanics, even Jews. Actually, it was originally to allow the white Europeans in! The church started, of course, in Israel and here was a case of a Roman officer and his friends, a group of Europeans, hearing the Gospel for the first time. Peter shared it with them, and then:

While Peter yet spake these words, the Holy Ghost fell on all them which heard the word. -- vs. 44

Amazing! The Gentiles began to praise God. The Jewish believers who were with Peter could hardly believe their eyes.

And they of the circumcision which believed were as-
tonished, as many as came with Peter, because that on
the Gentiles also was poured out the gift of the Holy
Ghost. -- vs. 45

This was something new to them. They had seen the Lord
witness to the occasional Gentile, as I pointed out earlier, but
by and large Christ's mission was to the Jews and was a fulfillment of Jewish prophecy and law. It had probably never
occurred to them that Gentiles could believe in the Jewish
Messiah.

It is thought-provoking that the church fathers in Jerusalem
took issue with Peter when he returned from his meeting with
Cornelius.

And when Peter was come up to Jerusalem, they that
were of the circumcision contended with him, Saying,
Thou wentest in to men uncircumcised, and didst eat
with them. -- Acts 11:2-3

It is as if they were saying, "Great fisherman, friend of Jesus,
you preached the sermon at Pentecost and led 3,000 people to
Christ! You were instrumental when 5,000 were saved at the
Temple gate. But still, you went into a Roman household, you
talked to Roman officers about Jesus Christ! Do you think
Gentiles can hear this and understand it and come to our Jewish Messiah?" So Peter explained the dream that God sent to
teach him that he should not call anything unclean:

But the voice answered me again from heaven, What
God hath cleansed, that call not thou common. -- vs. 9

Obviously, God had extended the Gospel to the Gentiles. There is actually a proof text for it. There is a certain game I play in churches that I visit. I say to people, "You're so certain of Gentile salvation. Give me a verse that tells me that Gentiles can be saved. I have a thousand verses in the Gospels that say Jews can be saved." They think it is almost a joke, and yet they cannot find a verse to support Gentile salvation. Try this one:

When they heard these things, they held their peace, and glorified God, saying, Then hath God also to the Gentiles granted repentance unto life. -- vs. 18

It is that simple. Gentiles are invited. Everyone is invited. When John the Baptist saw Jesus coming, he said, "Behold the Lamb of God, which taketh away the sin *of the world*" (John 1:29). Not *of Israel*, which would have been logical for him to say, since only Israel was under the law. No, salvation in Christ is for all, the death of Christ was for all, and the whole wide world is forgiven through the sacrifice of Christ. In this passage in Acts, we see it as it was starting to happen. This is the beginning of the history of Gentile salvation, at the home of Cornelius in Caesarea, a city located along the Mediterranean coast north of Tel Aviv and south of Haifa. The ruins of this city are still there and we visit them on our tours of Israel.

After the Jerusalem Christians had heard Peter's report and accepted that God's salvation is also for the Gentiles, the very next verse says:

Now they which were scattered abroad upon the perse-

cution that arose about Stephen travelled as far as
Phenice, and Cyprus, and Antioch, preaching the word
to none but unto the Jews only. -- vs. 19

Stephen was the Apostle who was stoned in Jerusalem. The
Messianic Jews were hated and feared by the Temple priest-
hood, which persecuted and scattered the young church. The
Christians on the road did not know about the conversion of
Cornelius and Peter's report to Jerusalem, so they continued
to preach only to the Jews. When they came to a town, they
would go to its synagogue. Paul did this throughout his career. When he arrived in Athens, he witnessed at the synagogue. In Asia, or what we call Turkey today, in the towns of
the seven churches and others that Paul visited, he went first
to the Jews, who would be interested to hear a rabbi from
Israel -- especially if he could report that the Messiah had come.
At the least, they would want to evaluate such a claim. The
Greeks would have no interest in this subject. So the scattered
believers took the Gospel first to the Jews alone. And a few
verses later in Acts 11, we find that:

. . . the disciples were called Christians first in Antioch.
-- vs. 26

If they were called "Christians" first in Antioch, and if the
people that went to Antioch were "preaching the word to none
but unto the Jews only" (Acts 11:19), then all the people who
were first called Christians were Jews! So, when the history
of Gentile salvation started, there were already many Christian Jews. The Christian church was well underway by the
time Cornelius and his household were saved.

About this time, the great missionary Paul was converted and set about spreading the Gospel and establishing churches throughout the Roman empire. Christianity grew until, a few centuries down the road, a major error came into the church. St. Augustine wrote a treatise called *The City of God*, in which he concluded that God was through with Israel and the church was its replacement. This was the start of replacement theology as a church doctrine.

Did Augustine write this out of malice or anti-Semitism? Did he dislike the Jews? Not necessarily. The Jews had been dispersed. The Romans raided Israel in 70 A.D. and again in 135 A.D. and the Jews fled far and wide. At the time of Augustine, there just was not a Jewish Israel to be seen. Even the name of the land was changed in 135 A.D. to Palestine — "Philistia," after the Philistines. (This name had nothing whatsoever to do with Arab peoples. The Moslems weren't to come on the scene for 500 years. The Romans renamed the land to wipe out Judaism. It was another of those "final solutions" to the Jewish problem. Today, we are hearing the preposterous idea that Arab Moslems are the original Palestinians. This is not only nonsense, it is crazier than nonsense.)

It wasn't long before the church picked up on Augustine's doctrine, and the original Catholic church began to think that it was Israel. This belief became a tenet of the church and was carried down through the centuries. However it started, it became an anti-Jewish doctrine which cut Israel and the Jews completely out of Christianity, even though they were the original Christians!

Roman Catholicism eventually led to the Reformation. Martin Luther called on fellow Christians to return to the Scriptures. And some of them did. They realized that the Scriptures were better than priests selling indulgences, and crusades and inquisitions, and other unbiblical burdens. But even though they returned to the Scriptures, somehow they continued the error of replacement theology. To them, the Jews were just some people who lived in the ghetto on the wrong side of town. Having been raised to view them as a disadvantaged minority with nothing to say about Christ, the Gentile Christians could not believe that they ought to seriously consider Israel. By the time of the Reformation, Israel as a country had not been in existence for almost 1500 years. It seemed like forever since Jews lived in the land.

And so the error of replacement theology continued. Over time, Christians split into denominations, with each one splintering into other sects until there are now something like 300 Christian denominations just in America. (One of the hard things in witnessing to Jews is when they ask, "Just which brand of Christianity would you like me to embrace?" That's a tough question.) But lately, there has been a new movement. I would almost call it a new Reformation or a neo-Reformation which has given birth to what are called "Bible churches." These churches get back to verse-by-verse study of the Scriptures. The Rapture has been uncovered and a greater theological understanding has come out of this. These churches reject replacement theology. They are actively involved with Israel. They have read the prophecies and are excited by the fact that God has brought the Jews back to the land.

Israel is crucial. It is God's timepiece. The true Bible churches study the Scriptures and not old doctrines, and so they avoid mistakes like replacement theology. They read the Abrahamic Covenant correctly:

> *And I will establish my covenant between me and thee and thy seed after thee in their generations for an ever-lasting covenant, to be a God unto thee, and to thy seed after thee. And I will give unto thee, and to thy seed after thee, the land wherein thou art a stranger, all the land of Canaan, for an everlasting possession; and I will be their God. -- Genesis 17:7-8*

When God established an "everlasting" covenant, it is impossible to say that somewhere down the line the Jews misbehaved and caused the covenant to be broken. God Himself said, "*olam*," which means "everlasting" in Hebrew. It is forever, complete, done, universal.

God's promise included all the land of Canaan. This is the sort of promise that those who study the Bible can appreciate. God means something when He says "everlasting." It will not vary; it will not end. Even though the Jews were later dispersed from the land, we are seeing the fulfillment of God's covenant today:

> *That then the LORD thy God will turn thy captivity, and have compassion upon thee, and will return and gather thee from all the nations, whither the LORD thy God hath scattered thee. If any of thine be driven out unto the outmost parts of heaven, from thence will the LORD thy God gather thee, and from thence will he fetch thee: And the LORD thy God will bring thee into the land which thy fathers possessed, and thou shalt*

possess it; and he will do thee good, and multiply thee
above thy fathers. -- Deuteronomy 30:3-5

No one -- no one! -- can read that passage and look at Israel
and not think, "those two go together." I don't care if he is the
latest theologian to write about replacement theology, he cannot escape this promise. There is a compelling parallel between God saying, "Even if you were driven to the outmost
parts of heaven" (that is, all over creation) and the phenom-
enon today of Jews being brought back to the land from Ethio-
pia, from Russia, from America, from South America, from
practically everywhere but the South Pole. If you think that
there is no correspondence between these two occurrences,
you might as well just throw the Bible away.

The dry bones vision in Ezekiel 37 also backs this up:

Then he said unto me, Son of man, these bones are the
whole house of Israel: behold, they say, Our bones are
dried, and our hope is lost: we are cut off for our parts.

Therefore prophesy and say unto them, Thus saith the
Lord GOD; Behold, O my people, I will open your
graves, and cause you to come up out of your graves,
and bring you into the land of Israel.

And ye shall know that I am the LORD, when I have
opened your graves, O my people, and brought you up
out of your graves,

And shall put my spirit in you, and ye shall live, and I
shall place you in your own land: then shall ye know

that I the LORD have spoken it, and performed it, saith the LORD. -- vss. 11-14

God says, "You're out there in Gentile lands, but I will open those graves and bring you back." That is a powerful image. "You thought you were dying out there, and I will bring you back into your own land, make you spiritual again, and then the kingdom will come." That is the point of the dry bones vision. Bone connects to bone, flesh to flesh as they build up. Then they take a breath, and the spirit comes into them, and they are whole. They are the true Israel restored.

We are in the middle of this today. We are seeing it happen. If someone says, "Israel doesn't count," it does not matter how many degrees he has, either he has to be wrong or the Bible is wrong. This is very personal with God. His love for Israel is not a casual thing. Defending Israel against mindless media bias, against the Moslems, especially against the replacement theologians, is very important to me and should be important to every believer. Israel will be our kingdom! We are going there for a thousand years. You could spend your whole life saying, "Israel doesn't count, Israel doesn't count," but you will end up standing there in Jerusalem with your King.

If Israel's behavior was bad, does it mean that God would turn His back on them? They disobeyed God out in the wilderness. The context in Leviticus 26 is chastisements, one after another:

But if ye will not hearken unto me, and will not do all these commandments; And if ye shall despise my stat-utes, or if your soul abhor my judgments, so that ye will not do all my commandments, but that ye break my covenant . . . -- Leviticus 26:14-15

God is angry. But, beginning in verse 44, He says:

And yet for all that, when they be in the land of their enemies, I will not cast them away, neither will I abhor them, to destroy them utterly, and to break my covenant with them: for I am the LORD their God. But I will for their sakes remember the covenant of their ancestors, whom I brought forth out of the land of Egypt in the sight of the heathen, that I might be their God: I am the LORD. -- vss. 44-45

God's covenant with Israel does not depend on their behavior, just as our salvation in Christ does not depend on our behavior. God is not keeping score and trying to keep people out. To be accurate, He said that He is not willing that any should perish (2 Peter 3:9). He is trying to get people in, for heaven's sake! His love for Israel, His forbearance with them, is unshakable.

There is no stronger passage about God's love for Israel than Jeremiah's announcement of the New Covenant:

Thus saith the LORD, which giveth the sun for a light by day, and the ordinances of the moon and of the stars for a light by night, which divideth the sea when the waves thereof roar; The LORD of hosts is his name. . . . -- Jeremiah 31:35

God gives these ordinances and signs this covenant, and He

says this:

> *If those ordinances depart from before me, saith the*
> *LORD, then the seed of Israel also shall cease from*
> *being a nation before me for ever. -- vs. 36*

The moon is still coming up and the sun is still shining. The waves still run up on the beach, therefore Israel is still a nation before the Lord.

> *Thus saith the LORD; If heaven above can be mea-*
> *sured, and the foundations of the earth searched out*
> *beneath, I will also cast off all the seed of Israel for all*
> *that they have done, saith the LORD. -- vs. 37*

God presented a similar situation to Job: "where were you when I laid the foundations of the earth; when I laid the cornerstone of the earth?" (Job 38:4,6) If you can tell God how the earth is hung in space, then He will agree, "O.K., I will cast off Israel." He cannot say it more strongly. Yet there are Christian scholars teaching that God has cast off Israel. They are wrong. Not right, not medium, but dead wrong.

Some people believe that the modern nation of Israel is not the same nation as the Israel of biblical times, but it is the only nation in the world today that can trace by language, by religion, by prayers and songs and costumes -- by everything -- that it does go back to that era. The people of Israel are the most exact picture we have from biblical times. Americans go back only 200 years; Englishmen perhaps 800 to 1,000 years. Only Israel goes back those thousands of years to the Scriptures, saying the same words every Sabbath as written there

3,500 years ago. This is the biblical Israel and you cannot cast it out. God has not cast it out.

If God takes His promises away based on behavior, then sinners cannot count on salvation in Christ either. If He must keep His promises to Christians as His people, then He must keep His covenant with Israel as well.

Paul saw the error of replacement theology in his own time, and dealt with it in Romans 11:

> *I say then, Hath God cast away his people? God forbid. For I also am an Israelite, of the seed of Abraham, of the tribe of Benjamin. God hath not cast away his people which he foreknew. . . . -- Romans 11:1-2*

The whole chapter of Romans 11 is devoted to this very error. I wonder if replacement theologians tear this chapter out of the Bible and refuse to read it. "God hath not cast away His people which He foreknew." If He hath, tell me how He hath! I like the note for this chapter in the Scofield Study Bible: "That Israel has not been forever set aside is the theme of this chapter."

If Israel has not been "forever set aside," then what is its current relationship to God? The coming of Jesus obviously brought changes in God's dealings with His people. A right relationship with God is now available only through the salvation provided by Christ's death and resurrection. Hebrews 8:13 makes clear that a new covenant has been established and the old one is obsolete. But what is the covenant that was actually done away with? This is the source of a lot of the confusion of replacement theology. God in fact established two covenants with Israel: the Abrahamic and the Mosaic. The Abrahamic covenant created the nation of Israel with Abraham as its father. The Mosaic covenant established the Law that would govern Israel. It is this second covenant that has been replaced by the new covenant in Christ:

> *For if that first covenant had been faultless, then should no place have been sought for the second.*
>
> *For finding fault with them, he saith, Behold, the days come, saith the Lord, when I will make a new covenant with the house of Israel and with the house of Judah:*
>
> *Not according to the covenant that I made with their fathers in the day when I took them by the hand to lead them out of the land of Egypt; because they continued not in my covenant, and I regarded them not, saith the Lord. -- Hebrews 8:7-9*

God's covenant with Abraham still stands and is active even today. In the supplementary materials at the end of this publication is an article by Dr. Thomas McCall, our staff theologian, which details God's present covenantal relationship with the nation of Israel. Israel also has a specific role to fulfill in End Times prophecy. I would refer you to other materials available through Zola Levitt Ministries that deal with prophecy and End Times events.

Many sincere Christians have been influenced by replacement theology, which leads to a twisted understanding of Scripture. In the supplementary articles, I have included a series of responses to a pastor's letter dealing with a request by a member of his congregation to attend a Passover seder. In his rebuke to this church member, the pastor demonstrates many of the errors that result from replacement theology. If God is indeed through with Israel, then Jewish traditions are obsolete and have no meaning, the Old Testament has no real value, and even Jews are no longer Jews. This line of reasoning doesn't fit with 2 Timothy 3:16-17, which states:

> *All Scripture is given by inspiration of God and is profitable for doctrine, for reproof, for correction, for instruction in righteousness: That the man of God may be perfect, throughly furnished unto all good works.*

When Paul wrote this, the New Testament had not yet been compiled, so the Scripture he was referring to was the Old Testament. God revealed Himself through those Scriptures for centuries in His dealings with Israel. God is the same, now and forever ("For I am the Lord, I change not." -- Malachi 3:6). To say that the Old Testament is obsolete implies that we can learn nothing from it, as if the God of Israel is not the same God we serve today. Our access to God has changed (through Christ rather than a high priest), but God Himself will never change.

Note the pastor's answer to the question of "who is a real Jew." He states that when a Jew turns to Christ "he becomes like all other Gentiles, he becomes a Christian believer. There are not two classes of believers in the New Testament." He has confused our spiritual relationship with God through Christ and God's covenantal relationship to Israel established through Abraham. As Christians, we are saved by grace alone, through faith, and stand in a right relationship with God because of Christ's sacrifice on the cross. As the pastor correctly states, there are not two classes of believers in God's sight. However, a Jew who turns to Christ does not become "like all other Gentiles," because God's covenant with Abraham still stands. And as a physical descendant of Abraham, the Christian Jew shares in that covenant. That is why many Messianic Jews refer to themselves as "completed Jews." Through the Abrahamic covenant, God established a special people to demonstrate Himself to mankind, a nation through which He would bring a Savior who would redeem the world. A Messianic Jew can appreciate his special heritage, seeing in Christ the redemption promised long ago through Abraham.

God still has plans for the people of Israel. There is a remnant faithful to God. There are Messianic congregations everywhere, and they believe the same Christian doctrine as any other congregation. The present national unbelief of Israel was foreseen. It is a matter of prophecy that Israel would be in unbelief; that should not surprise us. As a matter of fact, it opened up an opportunity for the Gentiles. Because of Israel's falling away, there was room for the Gentiles to come in. Israel is judicially broken off from the good olive tree called Christ, but they are to be grafted in again. Paul points out:

And they [Israel] *also, if they abide not still in unbelief, shall be grafted in: for God is able to graft them in again. For if thou wert cut out of the olive tree which is wild by nature, and were grafted contrary to nature into a good olive tree: how much more shall these* [Israel], *which be the natural branches, be grafted into their own olive tree? -- Romans 11:23-24*

The replacement theologians seem to believe that Gentile Christians were not just grafted in, but that the entire olive tree was uprooted and replaced!

Paul also teaches very simply in Romans 15 that if you have profited by the spiritual things of Israel, then support Israel in worldly things (Rom. 15:27). You can do that by talking to replacement theologians, showing them from the Scripture what their error is and admonishing them not to curse Israel. God said, "I will bless them that bless thee, and I will curse them that curse thee." We would be well advised to take that to heart.

The following article by our staff theologian appeared in the May 1993 **Levitt Letter.**

"What Advantage has the Jew?"
God's <u>Present</u> Covenantal Relationship with Israel
By Thomas S. McCall, Th.D.

Those of you who take this newsletter realize that we have been debating with Dallas Theological Seminary about their views on Israel. Since one of their professors expounded anti-Israel views on a Dallas talk show, their position has been unclear to this ministry. But recently we acquired a book edited by two of the professors and quoting other faculty which reveals their true position. Our ministry theologian, Dr. Thomas McCall, presents their ideas and his refutation in the article below.

After proving in the first two chapters of Romans that both Jews and Gentiles are lost as sinners and desperately in need of salvation, the Apostle Paul asks a natural question, *"Then what advantage has the Jew?"* (Rom. 3: ABV).

If Jews are just as lost in sin as Gentiles, it would appear that whatever advantages Jews may have enjoyed before, now that Christ has come and the Church has been created, one would think that unsaved Jews and Gentiles are on a completely level playing field, and that one group has no advantage over the other from God's point of view. We thus might mistakenly be led to answer Paul's question in the negative, and say "None, the unsaved Jews has no advantage over the unsaved Gentile." We would be wrong.

To our surprise, Paul answers his question, *"Much every way, chiefly because unto them were committed the oracles of God."* Astonishingly, the apostle asserts that unsaved Jews have numerous advantages over unsaved Gentiles, and the primary advantage is that God has committed to the Jews His Word, both in writing and in preservation. Concerning unsaved Gentiles, however, Paul states the following:

"Wherefore, remember that ye, being in time past Gentiles...that at that time ye were without Christ, being aliens from the commonwealth of Israel, and strangers from the covenants of promise, having no hope, and without God in the world" (Eph. 2:11-12).

The Apostle Paul, the apostle to the Gentiles, taught that there was a distinct, covenantal difference between unsaved Jews and unsaved Gentiles. It is only in Christ that there is no difference between Jews and Gentiles. Once we receive Christ and are placed into the Church, the middle wall of partition is removed, but outside of Christ there remains a great covenantal difference between unsaved Jews and unsaved Gentiles. Thus, he described humanity in three parts, *"the Jews, the Gentiles and the Church of God"* (1 Cor. 10:32).

By and large, Christianity reaffirmed this distinction between Jews and Gentiles outside of Christ during the early centuries of the Church Age. However, with leading writers like Eusebius and Augustine, there was a decided shift in thinking. These church leaders began to teach that the distinct covenantal relationship between God and Israel has been terminated. This led them to assert that the future promises to Israel, including the future Millennium, were now null and void, or have been somehow transferred to the Church.

This has been the predominant (and practically the only) view of scholarly Christianity through the Dark Age, the Reformation, and up until this present century. Around the turn of the century, some Christian leaders began to rediscover the uniqueness of Israel in the plan and purpose of God. It is notable that the rise of interest in Israel in the Church was very much parallel in time with the rise in Zionism among the Jews. Did one give birth to the other, or were they totally separate phenomena?

At any rate, various teachers of the Word taught that there was a biblical distinction between the Jews, the Gentiles and the Church, and that there was yet a national future for Israel, known as the Millennium, during which Christ will reign on earth along with the resurrected Church and with the regathered and saved Israel. Such a minority view within the church took on the names "premillennial," because of the belief that Christ would return before the millennium, and "dispensational," because of the view that God's dealings with humanity through the ages have progressed through well-defined periods called dispensations, such as Law and Grace. Critics have accused them of stating that these dispensations were different ways of salvation, but they consistently taught that the only way of salvation in all of the dispensations has been by grace through faith.

Names associated with this movement are Darby, Scofield, Moody, Chafer, Walvoord, Feinberg, Pentecost, Talbot, Unger, Ryrie, Lindsey, Campbell and numerous others during the past century or so. Dr. Ryrie, in *Dispensationalism Today*, explained that the most essential element in dispensationalism was the recognition of the distinction between the Church and Israel. Any confusion on this distinction would ultimately lead back to a denial of the Millennium and a return to the traditional amillennial Church doctrine.

One of the leading institutions defending dispensationalism and premillennialism for most of the twentieth century has been Dallas Theological Seminary. Out of its halls has come a great body of literature proclaiming the great truths of the Word of God, and numerous graduates have gone forth preaching Christ to the ends of the earth. *Time Magazine* once described Dallas Seminary as the "fortress of fundamentalism." I personally have always been greatly honored to embrace Dallas Seminary as one of my alma maters, where I was privileged to earn the doctorate in Old Testament Studies under Dr. Unger and Dr. Ryrie.

Now, however, there appears to be a new breed of scholars at this renowned seminary, who are openly repudiating the views of their institutional and spiritual forbearers. Zondervan has recently published a book entitled *Dispensationalism, Israel and the Church*. It is a compilation of chapters by various scholars from around the country, brought together and edited by Blaising and Bock. Dr. Craig A. Blaising is Professor of Systematic Theology at Dallas Theological Seminary, and Dr. Darrell L. Bock is Professor of New Testament Studies at Dallas Theological Seminary.

After extensively explaining that the essential element of dispensationalism (as defined by Dr. Ryrie) is a recognition of the distinction between Israel and the Church, Dr. Blaising proceeded to state that this entire approach was inadequate and too narrow. He thus disassociates himself from the earlier dispensationalism taught by Ryrie, Scofield and many others. Rather, he maintains, what is called for is a "progressive dispensationalism," which minimizes the distinctions between Israel and the Church.

Dr. Blaising further describes "the present dispensation, in which divine blessings of the Spirit are going to Jews and Gentiles equally while national blessings are in abeyance." The implication is that, outside of Christ during the Church Dispensation, Jews and Gentiles have equal standing before God, and that any national blessings regarding Israel have been suspended.

Is this view scriptural? As we saw in the opening of our article, there is a great distinction to this day between the status of the unsaved Jews and the unsaved Gentiles of the world. The Jewish people are seen to have a considerable advantage over the Gentiles in their exposure to the Old Testament Word of God. (Of course, Jews and Gentiles who have been exposed to the Gospel through Christian parents or friends would have a yet greater advantage than Jews or Gentiles who have not had that exposure.) Therefore, it cannot be maintained that divine blessings are going to Jews and Gentiles equally in this age. It is only within the Body of Christ that true equality exists between Jews and Gentiles, and we are made one in Him.

Furthermore, the national blessings for Israel are not in "abeyance." True, the Millennium has been postponed until after the Church Dispensation, but that is not the only blessing God has promised to Israel. There are many other covenantal blessings that are being provided for Israel now, <u>in this present dispensation</u>, which are not promised to any Gentile nation. Some of these blessings are enumerated as follows:

1. **Preservation.** God has promised to preserve Israel nationally to the end of time. There are many Gentile nations that have risen and fallen around Israel, but the Jews continue to survive as a distinct people. Some of the most strenuous efforts to destroy Israel have occurred during the Church Age (some, regrettably, at the hand of professing Christians), but Israel persists miraculously. This is a blessing which continues for Israel, but God has never made such a promise to any other nation.

2. **Believing Remnant During Church Age.** Another blessing God has promised to Israel is that there would always be a believing remnant in every age (Rom. 11:5). Just as in Elijah's time, so in the Church Age, there is a perennial remnant of believing Jews according to the election of grace. God made no such promise to any of the Gentile nations. We are grateful that people of many nations are coming to Christ, but God is under no obligation to save individuals of any particular Gentile nation. We can be assured, though, that there will never come a time when no Jews are saved.

3. **Oracles of God.** As indicated above, the chief advantage the Jews have is that God has committed to them His Word (Rom. 3:1,2). When God desired to bring His revelation to the world, He chose Israel to convey it. Jews are the writers of both the Old and New Testaments. Also, they are the continuing proclaimers of at least part of the Word of God. The first

Church conference was concerned about the sensibilities of Jews around the world, since Moses was "read in the synagogues every sabbath day" (Acts 15:21).

4. Of Whom, As Concerning the Flesh, Christ Came.

The crowning glory of Israel is that when God became a man, He became a Jew. The world, and even some Christians, may wish to forget this, but Satan never has. In the vision of Revelation 12, the dragon (Satan) ruthlessly attacks the woman (Israel) who gave birth to the Christ. Only Israel, among the nations, has the honor and blessing from God to claim that they are the progenitors of the Holy One of God, according to the flesh (Rom. 9:5). Satan hates Israel for this, and we who believe in Christ must not join Satan in such hatred.

5. The Reciprocal Blessing.

When God called Abraham, He told him, *"I will bless them that bless thee, and curse him that curseth thee"* (Gen. 12:3). This national blessing has never been revoked and continues in effect to this day. Those who bless Israel find themselves blessed by God, while those who curse the Jews sooner or later earn the curse of the Almighty.

6. Promise of Restoration to the Land.

One of the great national promises to Israel is that the Jewish people would be returned to their original land. This promise is repeated over and over again throughout the Scriptures (Amos 9:15), and to what else could Paul be referring when he reminds us Gentile Christians that to Israel pertains "the promises" (Rom. 9:4)? For nineteen centuries this national blessing certainly did seem to be "in abeyance," as the Jewish people found themselves in the often devastating dispersion among the Gentile nations. But in our generation, one of the most remarkable ethnic miracles of all time is occurring before our very eyes. Over four million Jews have returned to the Land, more than at any time in their history. If we who claim to believe the Word of God turn our backs on this astonishing development and say it means nothing, we would seem to have less spiritual discernment than those who ignored the first coming of the Messiah!

7. **Under the Law.** Paul said that to those who are under the law, he became as one under the law, that he might gain those who are under the law (1 Cor. 9:20). He considered that the Jewish people are still under the law, even in the current Church Age. We who are under grace and not under the law might wonder how much of a blessing this is, but compared to the Gentile nations, who have nothing, to be under the law is a great national blessing. The Law, the Torah, has been the guiding light for the people of Israel for all these centuries. How many Jews have been martyred, holding the scroll of the law to their breasts, crying aloud the immortal Shema, "Hear O Israel, the Lord our God, the Lord is one"? The Law is a schoolmaster to Christ, and many Jews through the centuries have come to know Christ through the Law. To have the Law is an important national blessing for Israel, which has continued throughout this dispensation without abatement. The Jewish Law is the only effective international law in operation today.

8. **Discipline from God.** The writer of Hebrews states that one way we can know that we are true sons of God is that we are chastened, or disciplined by Him. This is true of the Church, and it is also true of Israel. In His covenantal relationship with Israel, God has continually manifested discipline in the following ways:

    a. Dispersed from the Land (Luke 21:24)

    b. Without the Temple, sacrifice or priesthood (Hosea 3:4)

    c. Preserved through the persecutions of the Dispersion (Amos 9:15)

    d. Restored to the Land, initially in unbelief in Christ, as "dry bones" (Ezek. 37:12)

    e. Prepared to receive Jesus as their Messiah through "the Time of Jacob's Trouble," the Tribulation, and through the witness of 144,000 Israeli believers in Christ (Rev. 7)

    f. National salvation of Israel at the Second Coming of Christ (Rom. 11:26)

9. **Exhortation to Church.** There are several exhortations that the Apostle Paul gave to the Church about Israel. These exhortations show that the Church must consider Israel to be distinct in God's dealings from the vast Gentile world.

    a. Gentile believers in Christ are not to boast against the Jews, just because they have replaced unbelieving Jews in God's redemptive favor (Rom. 11:18).

    b. Gentile believers are urged to provoke the Jews to jealousy for their own Messiah (Rom. 11:11).

    c. The Church is urged to follow Paul's example of considering the Jews as primary candidates for the Gospel (Rom.1:16).

    d. The churches among the Gentiles are urged to support financially the "mother church" in the land of Israel, from which they have received so much spiritual benefit (Rom. 15:26-27).

e. The Church was to recognize that the current blindness of Israel is partial and temporary, and that all Israel (the Jewish people who survive the Tribulation) will be saved when Christ returns (Rom. 11:25-26).

f. The Church is to understand that even though unbelieving Jews are now enemies of the Gospel, the nation Israel is still loved by God for the sake of His covenant with the fathers, Abraham, Isaac and Jacob (Rom. 11:28).

With all of this evidence, how can we say that the national blessings to Israel are in abeyance in the Church Age? On the contrary, God's covenantal relationship with Israel is just as strong and in effect now as it ever has been. We urge the evangelical Church, and especially all who consider themselves to be dispensationalists, to reject this effort of "progressive dispensationalism" to deny the important distinctions between Israel and the Church. We must return to the sound biblical roots of our spiritual forefathers of recent times and of the Apostolic era, and reject any attempt to accommodate with the false notions and unbiblical views of non-dispensationalists and amillennialists.

We must always love the brethren in Christ, but we cannot compromise the faith once and for all delivered to the saints for the sake of apparent unity.

The following article appeared in two installments in the September 1994 and October 1994 **Levitt Letter.** *It is part of a series of articles on the history behind the recent restoration of the land of Israel.*

Israel
The Center of Divine History
Parts IV & V
By Thomas S. McCall, Th.D.

Pro-Zionist Christianity, which developed in the latter part of the 19th century along with Zionism, played a significant role in the beginnings of Israel, as we shall see, at the time of World War I. They accomplished this mainly through the politics of the time in England and America. However, all Christian leaders did not espouse pro-Zionist Christianity, which was based primarily on the newly revived Premillennial/Dispensational theology. While they were energetic and vocal, the Premillennial/Dispensational Christians were (and continue to be) in the minority. Most professing Christians in Europe and in the American Hemisphere have long held the opposing view of Amillennial/Postmillennial Christianity.

Anti-Zionist Christianity

While there are some subtle distinctions between Amillennialism and Postmil-lennialism concerning any future for Israel, they are the same. They teach that any covenant relationship God had with Israel was cancelled at the time of the First Coming of Christ. Therefore, God is through with the Jewish people as a nation, and there is to be no State of

Israel, now or in the future. In addition, there is to be no Temple, and no Millennial Kingdom for Israel with Jerusalem as its capital. Any blessings to the Jewish people must be along with all other nationalities under the aegis of the Church. Furthermore, God has transferred and transformed to the Church all the blessings and promises He originally made to Israel. Thus, the Church is the New Israel.

Scholars sometimes call this view Replacement Theology, as it views the Church as replacing Israel in all aspects. In contrast, the Premillennial/Dispensational view is that, while the Church is the new creation of the Lord that proclaims the Gospel in this age, the Church does not replace Israel in its national covenant relationship with God. The covenant with Israel does not guarantee personal salvation for all Jews. It does, though, guarantee personal salvation for the "remnant" of Jewish people in all ages, including the Church Age. Also, it guarantees the preservation and restoration of Israel to the Land in preparation for the Tribulation and the second Coming of Christ.

Because of these theological convictions, then, the Amillennial/ Postmillennial Christians tend to look at any idea of a future for Israel with alarm, as an affront to Christianity, as a denial of the true position of the Church. The Premillennial/ Dispensationalists, on the other hand, view the idea of a future for Israel with delight. Modern Israel is a welcome harbinger of the Rapture of the Church and the second Coming of Christ.

What does the New Testament teach — Premillennialism or Replacement Theology? There is not as much disagreement about this as one might suppose. Most of the Replacement

Theologians and Amillennialists agree with the Premillennialists that the New Testament apostles believed in a future for Israel and the literal second Coming of Christ — but they say the apostles were just mistaken! It took time for the Church to "mature" to the knowledge that Christ was not returning to the earth, and that Israel was to be replaced by the Church.

Augustine and Replacement Theology

It was Augustine around A.D. 400 who ultimately articulated the idea, principally in his well-known work, *The City of God.* Augustine admitted that at one time he had espoused the doctrine of "Chiliasm," the belief in a future millennium, in which the Church and redeemed Israel will be blessed by the personal return and reign of Christ on the earth. However, he had since come to the "more satisfactory" view that the Church has replaced Israel forever. Jerusalem and the Temple were destroyed in fulfillment of prophecy, and the Jews were dispersed throughout the Roman empire. Judaism was branded in the New Testament as an imperfect religion that has been superseded by the Gospel of Christianity. Rome was in its ascendancy as the center of Christian thought and worship.

Rather than looking to some political renewal on this present earth, Augustine taught that we should look to the New Jerusalem, the eternal city of God. In effect, he "leapfrogged" over the Millennium as a future event and saw the Millennial promises fulfilled in the Church age. He further envisioned the Second Coming of Christ as not ushering in the Millennium, but the Eternal State of the New Heaven, the New Earth, and the New Jerusalem.

Christendom canonized Augustine as an official saint, and theologians throughout the Roman Empire accepted his doctrines. The Chiliasts were branded as holding aberrant views, if not heresy, and Augustinian Replacement Theology became the cornerstone of Roman Catholic concepts. In the later developments in the Eastern Orthodox Church, the European Reformation and the Anglican split, Replacement Theology continued essentially untouched. It was an important part of the standard Christian view of Israel, the world, and prophecy.

The effect of all this on Christian attitudes about Israel was devastating. In actuality, Replacement Theology disenfranchised Israel from having a continuing covenant relationship with God. Instead of looking at Jerusalem as the "City of the Great King," in which Christ will reign for a thousand years upon His return, they saw Jerusalem's perpetual desolation as much as a confirmation of Christianity as the destruction of Pharaoh's army in the Red Sea was a confirmation of Moses.

Dominance of Replacement Theology in Church History

This anti-Israel view continued as dominant in Christianity until the rise of Premillennial/Dispensationalism (along with Zionism) in the 19th Century. Replacement Theology is still the majority view among professing Christian theologians, but Premillennialism is by and large considered a legitimate and vocal minority, at least in evangelical Protestant circles.

Thus, in relation to the rise of Zionism and Modern Israel, Christianity has brought a divided message. Some (the Premillennial/Dispensationalists) have applauded the rise of the new State of Israel as evidence of the near fulfillment of the Second Coming of Christ. However, many representatives of official Christianity (the Replacement Theologians) are either neutral or antagonistic.

Christianity Both Pro- and Anti-Israel

Such organizations as the Roman Catholic Church and the World Council of Churches have, for the last half century, taken positions favoring the Arab and Moslem enemies of Israel. They have defended this bias partly by claiming representation in the various countries involved. But a vital part of this bias is based on the theological convictions that cannot abide the resurrection of Israel from the ashes of the Dispersion.

It is with considerable reluctance that the Vatican has recognized Israel, and the Church's primary interest is in asserting its influence in maintaining its Holy Places in Jerusalem. Similarly, the World Council of Churches has consistently pled the cause of Palestinians against the claims of Israel.

Thus, Christianity has, because of its differing theological views about the future of Israel, had a divided attitude about Zionism and the revived State of Israel. Part of Christianity has expressed delight with the modern Israel, while part has been very negative toward Israel's very existence.

A Practical Case

The following letters and articles appeared in the March 1995 and May 1995 Levitt Letter.

Letters to Zola

We recently received a letter from a Messianic Jewish supporter who had invited his pastor to a Passover Seder in his home. The pastor declined with the following letter.

You asked me the other day if I wouldn't join with you for your Passover Seder next April. I must say, my brother, that it makes me concerned to hear anybody put so much emphasis on the old Jewish traditions that were very clearly done away with and have no value.

We're delighted that God has led you to attend _____. We are a New Testament church which holds the word of God in high esteem, both the Old and New Testaments, but we understand that the Old Testament has no value to us at this time, only as a type and shadow to lead us to a better covenant.

I am sure you are very sincere in walking through these Old Testament rituals, but they can also be very divisive if we make them the center of our life, as I feel you might be doing. Even your Jewish dress sends a signal to the church that you are different than them, which I could not accept from a biblical standpoint. When a man accepts Jesus Christ it eliminates all nationalities and is no longer a racial issue. There is no bond or free, Jew or Gentile in the body of Christ. The blood of Christ, the final sacrifice, has been paid. I know that some people have wondered about your emphasis on the Jewish traditions rather than to accept the Christian church traditions. This could be very offensive to some since those things have been done away with in Christ.

Hebrews 8 tells us that we have a better covenant established on better promises and if the first covenant with all its ordinances and rituals was sufficient, there would have been no need for the new covenant. I think in some ways if we keep focusing on the old covenant and its rituals, we send a signal to at least some that the New Covenant is not complete and yet, Hebrews 8:13 says that we have a new covenant and the first is obsolete and is old and vanishes away.

Colossians 2:14 tells us, "Having wiped out the handwriting of the requirements that were against us which were contrary to us." Verses 16-17 tell us, "So let no one judge you in food or in drink, or regarding a festival or a new moon or Sabbaths, which are a shadow of things to come, but the substance is of Christ." Verses 20-23, "Therefore if you have died with Christ from the basic principles of the world, why, as though living in the world, do you subject yourselves to regulations —do not touch, do not taste, do not handle, which all concern things which perish with the using — according to the commandments and doctrines of men? These things indeed have an appearance of wisdom in self-imposed religion, false humility, and neglect of the body, but are of no value against the indulgence of the flesh."

I personally believe that it is an offense to God to go

back into the Old Testament and try to resurrect all the ceremonies and feasts that have been done away with in Christ as he is the ultimate fulfillment. I am sure you are very sincere in wanting to talk about the types but we are not under those types any more. We should come into a new covenant relationship and establish our fellowship, not based upon the Old Testament's ritual, but the New Testament covenant. Passover is fulfilled every time we go to the table of the Lord. I don't want to go back to the Jewish Passover and imitate that which has vanished away.

I hope you will take this letter in the love that I am writing it. I am simply saying that in _____ we are not going to follow this nor do we want our people to be involved with this kind of Old Testament teaching. You are most welcome to be part of the _____ family if this is your desire, but we do not want you to bring the Jewish customs into the body and make that the basis of fellowship. Thank you for your cooperation while attending and becoming part of this house.

May God richly bless you as we spread the gospel of Jesus Christ in its purity in our Jerusalem, Samaria, Judea and the uttermost parts of the world.

Dear Pastor:

G.G., of your congregation, has written to this ministry and forwarded to me the letter that you sent to him about your thoughts on Old Testament and the Passover service. Obviously, your rebuke breaks the heart of any Jew and would be amazing to the Lord Himself, who commemorated all Jewish festivals and quoted the Old Testament voluminously.

The enclosed videotape on Gentile salvation refutes replacement theology, a position you evidently must hold, and I hope you will prayerfully consider its logic. I have used Scripture throughout to back up what I have said, and I hope you will open-mindedly view the program.

May I say in closing that those of us who make it our work to witness of Jesus Christ to the Jews — His own ministry — find it awfully difficult in light of the sort of ideas you expressed in your letter. I will be featuring your letter (without names or places) in the March newsletter of this ministry with biblical refutation by our resident theologian, Dr. Thomas S. McCall.

We disagree sharply, my brother, but we are neither Jew nor Greek in our love of our Lord. I would value your answer to the enclosed program.

In Christ's service, Zola

Why do Christians Have Passover Seders?
by Thomas S. McCall, Th.D.

This April in churches, Messianic congregations and homes all over this country and the world, Jewish and Gentile believers in Christ will be sitting down to a Passover feast. The setting is much the same as our Lord Jesus and His disciples had in Jerusalem the night before He died. Some Christian leaders have criticized this practice as putting emphasis on the Law of Moses and old Jewish traditions that were done away with and have no value.

Do we have the Passover meal because we think we are under the Law of Moses and are required to do so? Absolutely not! We who know the Messiah Jesus are not under the law, but under grace. We hold the Passover voluntarily. It's not something we <u>have</u> to do, but something we <u>want</u> to do, and the following are some of the reasons why.

To Know Christ Better

The more we know about the Passover, the more we will know about the Lord Jesus Christ Himself. Paul, the great Hebrew Christian apostle to the Gentiles, exhorted the church in Corinth:

Christ, our Passover, is sacrificed for us. Therefore, let us keep the feast ... with the unleavened bread of sincerity and truth (I Cor. 5:7-8).

Jesus is so identified with the Passover feast of the Jewish people that He is actually called "Christ our Passover." In other words, He is the Passover, He fulfills the Passover, and everything in the Passover speaks of Him and His redemptive work.

Undoubtedly, John the Baptist had this in mind when he introduced Yeshua (the original Hebrew name of Jesus) to the people of Israel, "Behold the Lamb of God who taketh away the sin of the world" (John 1:29). He was saying to Israel, here is God's Passover Lamb who will make atonement for our sins. If we are to understand Christ fully, we certainly have to understand the Passover feast and all that it means. How are we going to do this without actually observing what goes on at a Passover feast? That should be incentive enough for us. But there is more.

To Have a Deeper Appreciation
For the Lord's Supper

The Lord's Supper was established by Christ at the time of the Passover feast. Earlier that day He told His disciples to go and prepare the Passover in the Upper Room. That means they had to take the selected lamb to the Temple, sacrifice it to the Lord, leave a portion of it with the priests, and take the remainder of the lamb to the Upper Room where they prepared it along with the other items for the feast.

When they were assembled in that famous dining room in Jerusalem, Jesus told His disciples, "With desire I have desired to eat this Passover with you before I suffer" (Luke 22:15). Out of the Passover feast, He explained the deepest truths concerning His death the following afternoon, and gave us the

Lord's Supper to remember His death until He comes again. In a very real sense, whenever we observe the Lord's Supper, we are observing an abbreviated Passover feast. The more we know about the Passover, the more appreciation we will have for the ordinance of the Lord's Supper.

To Understand the Bible More Completely

The Passover is one among many of the great types of the Old Testament that are fulfilled in the New Testament. From the Passover feast come the great stories of the exodus of Israel out of bondage in Egypt, the dreadful night of life and death that first Passover night, the blood of the Passover lamb, the crossing of the Red Sea and the occupation of the Promised Land. These miraculous events foreshadowed the redemption provided by the Messiah.

Christ Jesus has taken us believers out of Egypt-like slavery to sin, through the Red Sea of identification with Him and into the Promised Land of spiritual victory. How limited would be our comprehension of what the Lord has done for us if it were not for the great historical events of the Exodus account in the Old Testament. The Passover feast is a tie that binds the Old and New Testaments together in type and fulfillment.

To Help Us Witness to Our Jewish Friends

Many Christians want to witness to Jewish people, but don't know where to begin. The Passover is a good starting point. It is very meaningful to Jewish families, and is observed every year in their homes. It is part of being a Jew to keep the Passover feast, as it has been for 3,500 years, since the time of

Moses.

If we who believe in the Lord also know and understand the Passover, it will give us a point of communication with our Jewish friends. We can begin with the traditional Passover and go on to the fulfillment of the feast in the Messiah, Christ Jesus, the Lamb of God. The Messianic congregations and churches that put on annual Passover banquets customarily invite the Jewish people of the community to share the feast with them. In this congenial and familiar atmosphere, many Jews have heard for the first time the way in which Jesus fulfills the ancient Passover. It would be difficult to calculate how many have come to the Lord in part through this kind of exposure to the Passover feast that not only portrays Moses, Israel and Egypt, but also the sacrifice of God's true Lamb.

We must not look on the Passover as an outmoded tradition that has faded into insignificance, but as a marvelous medium of edification for believers in Christ, and for evangelism among the lost sheep of the house of Israel.

Pharoah Rides Again!

Pharoah met his match in an argument over Passover with the God of Israel. Since that time, Gentiles seem to be sensitive about Jewish feasts and particularly this one, which our Lord so honored. Our regular readers will recall that we presented in the March issue a letter from a pastor rejecting a Passover invitation. One of our viewers, a Jewish believer, was rebuked by the senior pastor of his large church for the offense of wanting to include him in his Seder. The pastor declared such festivals "nailed to the cross."

We presented Dr. Thomas S. McCall's excellent observations on why Christians should know these feasts and how relevant they are to understanding our roots. The argument went on back at the church, however, and our viewer received counsel from two other ministries. We have reprinted their letters below, along with the pastor's newest reply. This time our anti-Jewish senior pastor friend presents some of this "theology" to back up his original rebuke. A third ministry wrote directly to the pastor after that. Finally, I have dealt with the pastor in an open letter at the end.

We run this correspondence, not in a spirit of dissension, but because there is a great deal to learn here. Anti-Semitism in today's Church is all too common and truly a very grave error. It is in regard to the unbelievers of the Antichrist's society in the Tribulation Period that the Lord warns Israel, "Ye shall be hated of all nations." This should never be true of any Christian believer.

Dear G.:

Shalom to you in our Messiah Jesus! I enjoyed our conversation Wednesday evening and I'm continuing to pray that God will grant you wisdom in dealing with your relationship with the Senior Pastor of your church and with people at the church in general. I'm sorry that you haven't experienced the kind of support that I know many Christians' pastors like to give to a Jewish believer who sincerely wants to express their Jewishness in the context of their faith in Christ. I pray that you will be able to find that kind of environment and will grow closer to the Lord Jesus through this experience. I need to qualify my remarks by saying that there may be certain things I'm not able to see or understand, not having been involved directly in this situation. Having only spoken to you and seeing the re-typed letter that you sent, it is hard for me to get a full picture. Also, because I don't know the church or the pastor personally, it's difficult to get a handle on the situation.

Basing what I'm saying on the principle of I Cor. 13:6, "love believes all things," I would like to believe what we have here is a misunder-standing or perhaps a misrepresentation of one another's viewpoints that may be cleared up. As I was saying on the phone, it seems to me if you want to approach the pastor in response to his letter, it would be best to do it in writing and it will be best to formulate your thinking in terms of asking for clarification rather than "sharing your views." I think it is important for you to also affirm to your pastor that you are fully in agreement with him on a number of points. For example, you should be able to affirm:

* that you, as a follower of Jesus the Messiah, are in relationship to God through the New Covenant which is es-

tablished in His shed blood;

   * *that you know that you are saved by grace, through faith, and not through observance of the Old Testament law;*

   * *that you are one with him and with all brothers and sisters in Christ and that you share a common family, a common hope and a common destiny as a member of the body of Christ.*

   Then you might lay some questions before him and ask him to explain what he means by several statements that he made. First of all he said, "when a man accepts Jesus Christ it eliminates all nationalities...." While we know that God is no respecter of persons and all of us who are in Christ are one, does he really think that national, cultural and gender distinctions are "eliminated?" We know that women still have roles within the family and within the church and it is still the women who are having the babies. Throughout the world there are a wide variety of cultural expressions within the Christian faith. There is no one, single "Christian culture." If we recognize that there is a black Christian cultural expression, a Chinese Christian cultural expression, couldn't there also be a legitimate Jewish Christian cultural expression? What did Paul mean when he said, "to a Jew I became as a Jew?"

   Secondly, could he please explain what he means by saying, "the Old Testament has no value to us at this time...?" Surely he doesn't mean that two-thirds of the Bible has no value. When Paul wrote to Timothy, "all Scripture is given by inspiration of God and is profitable for doctrine for reproof or correction for instruction in righteousness," he certainly wasn't excluding the Old Testament, was he? G., I would say to him,

"Pastor, I will be the first to criticize anyone who seeks to impose observance of any ceremonies or religious observances as being a requirement from God, necessary for salvation or a basis for fellowship. This would contradict the freedom that we have in Christ, but Pastor, if it is in fact freedom, then shouldn't I also be free, as a Jewish believer, to celebrate a Passover celebration that points to the fact that Jesus fulfilled this type in His death and resurrection? Much Christian literature has been written on these subjects, and on the observance or celebration of some of these festivals in light of their fulfillment in Christ. The authors portray this as an enriching experience that many well-known evangelical theologians, pastors and lay leaders have endorsed. I refer you to the following books as example of this kind of endorsement:

1.) "Christ in the Passover, Why is This Night different," by Ceil and Moishe Rosen, published by Moody Press;

2.) "Celebrate the Feasts," by Martha Zimmerman

Pastor, the last thing I want to do is cause controversy in the church. I don't want to be offensive and I'm afraid that perhaps I have been offensive to you, or to others who may misunderstand my intentions. I was born a Jew and I will die a Jew. When I came to Christ, I did not stop being Jewish. I became a completed Jew. My unbelieving Jewish family would very much like for me to say that I am no longer Jewish. That would confirm their belief that Jesus is not for them, since they are Jews.

Pastor, for most Jews, this is one of the main stumbling blocks to considering the gospel. We are told that faith in Christ makes us a gentile. Now you and I both know that faith in Christ doesn't make anyone become Jewish or gentile. It makes Jews and gentiles become Christians, followers of the resurrected Messiah. The fact that all of the first believers in Jesus were Jews, that they continued to live as Jews and often observed Jewish customs, should raise some questions as to whether or not there is a legitimate expression of Jewish Christian faith possible today.

Pastor, I don't want to be in a position of challenging you. I would like to believe that there has been some misunderstanding of my own convictions. Could you help me to understand if I've clarified some things or do you still feel that I am still thinking wrongly concerning these things? I value your wisdom and look forward to hearing from you. Sincerely in Christ."

G., feel free to use as much or as little of this as you would like. Once again, I thank you for allowing me to use your letter as a possible jumping off point for a Mishpochah Message sometime in the future. I'm sure what we eventually come up with will be quite a bit different than what I've given you in this letter. I didn't want to wait any longer in responding because I know that the issue is current for you. If you want to discuss any of these points, or if you have any questions, please don't hesitate to call or write. Also, if you do write to him along these lines, I would like the opportunity to see your letter and also to see your pastor's response, if he does respond. I am praying that God will give you wisdom as to how to proceed.

Shalom in Jesus, D. B., Jews for Jesus

Dear G.,

   Your letter regarding your church's misunderstanding of the Jewish roots of Christianity has been received and considered. This packet of information is sent in answer to your request for teachings which you can pass on to your pastor. It is hoped that the enclosed materials will give you scriptures and a perspective from which to address your Jewish understanding of the roots of our faith in Yeshua.

   You will find a study on the Levitical feasts of Israel, which describes the Biblical imperative to keep them, along with an explanation of how they have been or will be fulfilled by Messiah. The feasts are likened to rehearsals; as we observe them, or study the observance of each feast, we can better understand God's plan for salvation. We can come to a deeper and better understanding of God and who He is, as the Father and as the Son. We develop an appreciation of who Messiah is, why He came, and why He lived and spoke as He did, that becomes very real to us. Instead, He has created a system that _involves_ us in learning, making the learning much more effective. We actually eat the communion bread and drink the wine! Yeshua requires us to do this. He was just doing more of the same type of teaching He had done throughout Scripture. He also NEVER did away with Jewish traditions, but, as in the above example, He followed them throughout His life. Yeshua _did_ decry the traditions of men, but never those of God. Our Lord never changed; His requirements of us to remember what He did for us in the past were never done away with at Messiah's coming. Yeshua did not create the

"Christian church traditions" that your pastor refers to. Rather, it is documented in the New Testament that He observed the traditions of the Jewish culture at the time that were in accord with the Scriptures. He said that not a "jot or tittle" of the Scriptures was changed by Him. He provided fulfillment and life in the law, and a more complete understanding of the purposes of His commandments.

You will also find enclosed a brochure on Messianic Jews and a catalog rich in resources for teaching the Jewish roots of the Christian faith. Another good source is the book Our Father Abraham *by Marvin Wilson.*

I prayerfully hope this material gives you the insights you need to correct the mis-information your pastor exhibits. Please keep us informed as to the progress you make with him. Thank you for your desire to educate those in the church concerning the truth of God's design for His body of believers.

Sincerely in Messiah, C. M., Congregation Emmaus

_____

After receiving the above two letters of Christian counsel, G. wrote to his pastor, tactfully utilizing the polite expressions of those experienced witnesses to the Jews. The pastor replied to our viewer with the letter below.

Dear G.:

Grace and peace be unto you in the name of our Lord Jesus.

Thank you for your letter of February 28. I appreciate your clarification as to your view concerning the Old Testa-

ment and its prophetic fulfillment in the church of Jesus Christ.

I have no objection to anybody studying the Passover celebration and pointing out the fact that Jesus is the total and final fulfillment of it, as long as they are not trying to resurrect the Old Testament types and shadows, which according to Hebrews have decayed and been done away with.

I appreciate you not wanting to cause controversy in the church and I respect you for that. There have been churches that have been divided over this issue and we just didn't want it to start. We have a fellowshipping church in Bend, Oregon that became so involved in the extremes of the types and shadows that they actually made a religious form out of them, even to the extent that they began to meet on Saturday, which was the true Sabbath given to Moses. It became a very divisive issue and we did not want that to happen here at (our church).

One thing in your letter that I would like to clarify is our view of who is a real Jew. In the book of John, Jesus spoke to the Jews and said that unless they accepted Him they were not Jews, but were of their father the devil. In Hebrews he says that a person is not a Jew because of natural birth, but of spiritual birth. In Romans 11 the scriptures are very clear that when it comes to the fulfillment in Christ, that Jews of the Old Testament who did not accept Jesus Christ were branches broken off and they became Gentiles, or lost. Gentile simply means heathen, without God, without Christ. They became strangers to the covenant of promise, as it says in Ephesians 2. It goes on and says in Romans 11 that if they, speaking of the Jewish people, abide not in unbelief, they are able to be grafted back in again. They will be grafted in to the only thing you can be grafted into, the olive tree, which after Christ is made up of believers, Jew and Gentile. So when a Jew who is lost and bound for hell turns to Jesus Christ, he becomes like all other Gentiles, he becomes a Christian believer. There are not two classes of believers in the New Testament. Those that are not in Christ are not the true Jew. Perhaps they are Jews in the flesh, but not of the spirit, and the Bible says in Galatians 5 that we are the Israel of God who have had our hearts circumcised.

G., I feel that is the issue and if you could accept that issue I don't think you would have any problem at (our church). But if that issue is different then I think you will have problems. You may be a completed Jew, but that means you are a member of the body of Christ and there are neither Jew or Gentiles, bond or free in this house, we are all one in Christ.

I trust you understand our view and maybe this will be of help to you. I am going to take the liberty of sending a copy of this letter to my assistant pastor.

In His Name, your fellow-servant, Rev. D.I.

Dear Pastor,

Your letter addressed to your parishioner, Mr. G. G., was recently brought to my attention when it appeared in Dr. Zola Levitt's respected publication The Levitt Letter. As a Gentile woman who chairs a Messianic ministry, your terminology and arguments stated for discarding the Old Testament as nothing but an antiquated history of the Jewish people, rang all too familiar.

I am not some midwestern church lady who teaches Sunday school and who votes the straight Republican ticket. My entire career has been spent in motion picture production in Los Angeles and I served as the Assistant Director of Production Operations for Paramount Pictures. Before I woke up and smelled the bagels, I had been just as arrogant as you are about our Gentile copyright on the Jewish Messiah. The motion picture industry is directly responsible for your misconception of who Jesus really is. Hollywood has effectively turned Jesus into a Gentile complete with blue eyes, blonde hair, and a British accent. Jesus is big box office material.

My ministry has dedicated itself to celebrating the contributions made by both Jewish and Gentile women of the Bible to Christianity. I notice when you quote the famous statement of the Apostle Paul, "there is no bond or free, no Jew or Gentile, in the body of Christ," *you conveniently leave out the part about* "no male or female." *This kind of "sound byte" scripture quoting doesn't surprise me. Men like you have been using this technique for centuries to suppress women in the church from participating in the same liturgical privileges as men. It is no wonder you would use this same technique to sound-byte the entire Jewish race out of existence.*

From a theological standpoint if, as you say, the Jewish festivals were "nailed to the cross," why were Joseph of Aramathea, Mary Magdalene, and the entire entourage of Christians in attendance at the crucifixion in such an all fired hurry to get Jesus buried by sundown in order to keep a festival Sabbath which, according to your interpretation, had just been cancelled? When God commands a festival to be kept "forever" as an "everlasting ordinance," does He mean that "forever" ended at the cross? Maybe we've all passed into some cosmic dispensation outside the time frame of the Bible, and no one told me. Or maybe we're just caught in an episode of "Star Trek" and we've all been thrown into a time warp from which we can never escape. Funny, there was nothing about it on CNN!

Before a Jew brought me to the true Jewish Messiah, I was just as arrogant as you about my Gentile Christian superiority over the Jew. After all, we've got Jesus, all they've got is Moses, right? Your letter to Mr. G. seems more concerned with Christian conformity within your congregation than with Biblical accuracy. You no doubt celebrate Easter in lieu of Passover. I wonder if you even realize that Easter was originally a Roman fertility orgy in honor of a pagan goddess. Yet, with your Easter basket in hand, you proceed to nullify a festival designed by God Himself, and observed by Christ and the Apostles.

Our national organization applauds Mr. G.'s courage in the face of Christian anti-Semitism. If it were not for the Jews, we would have no Christian Messiah. We Gentiles would still be worshipping idols and baying at the moon, had the Jews not civilized us and taught us that God was not inside some clay statue of a bird or a cow. There seems to be one sound-byte scripture blatantly absent from your letter to Mr. G.: "...to the Jew first, and also to the Gentile," Romans 1:16.

Upon reading this letter, you have no doubt concluded that I am some left wing, feminist lesbian who believes that all white males are inherently evil. I am none of those things. I am, however, humbled and in awe of the sanctity of the Jewish Torah, the accuracy of the Jewish Prophets, the courage of the Jewish Apostles, and the sacrifice made by the Jewish Messiah. I am proud to be considered a "righteous Gentile" by my Jewish friends. I have been just as arrogant and just as ignorant as you in my self-righteous delusion that as a Gentile, I was somehow going to be moved up to the front of the line for entry into Heaven.

A Jew brought me to the true Messiah and I believe a Jew could explain to you the Jewish foundation upon which Christianity is built so that you might better understand your faith and the "fullness of the Gospel." Dr. Zola Levitt is an internationally renowned Biblical scholar who has produced comprehensive source materials on both the Old and New Testaments and how each relate to the other. As a fellow Gentile believer, I respectfully suggest you place your order immediately.

Before you start nullifying the covenants of God and replacing the Jewish people with your particular Gentile Brand of Christianity, look up at the sky the next time it rains. The rainbow covenant is still with us and so are God's chosen people.

Very truly yours, K.R.C.

After digesting all of the above, I wrote to the pastor as follows.

Dear Pastor,

In all good faith I have never heard such convoluted scriptural thinking. You do away with the Old Testament, and you try to prove Jews are really Gentiles. You quote a specific statement of our Lord's to a small group of Pharisees in one argument, and try to apply it to all Jews of all times. Supposing that Jews became Gentiles, then you rummage through the New Testament for scriptures meant to deny them even their relationship to Abraham and God's Covenant.

This is not even honest. My feeling is you dislike Jewish people and would prefer to cut them away from all things Christian. And that must be quite a job. If one dislikes, say Blacks or Hispanics or some other particular people, it would be hard enough to use the Bible to justify that prejudice. But if one hates the Jews, he is despising those whom God loves, the authors of the whole Bible, including the New Testament and the very brethren of Jesus Christ (Matt. 25:40).

Pastor, Jesus Christ is a Jew. He was then, He is now, and He will be when you face Him very soon.   — Zola

A current list of Zola Levitt's books, tapes, albums, videos, and other materials is available at no charge from:

ZOLA
P. O. Box 12268
Dallas, TX 75225-0268

STUDY BOOK SERIES by Zola Levitt

THE MIRACLE OF PASSOVER
A complete explanation of the beautiful symbols and shadows of the Messiah which appear in this crown jewel of Jewish Holy Days. The true meaning of Communion as the Lord instituted it and as the Church practices it.

THE SPIRIT OF PENTECOST
From the fear and trembling of the Upper Room to the magnificent miracle of the coming of the Holy Spirit. An exciting presentation of the full meaning of "the birthday of the Church."

A CHRISTIAN LOVE STORY
The Jewish wedding customs of the Messiah's time and how He fulfilled them all in calling out His Bride, the Church. A new and deeper understanding of the bond between the Bridegroom and each believer — a spiritual "Love Story."

THE SIGNS OF THE END
The Messiah's own words of warning about the conditions that would prevail in the world at the end of God's plan. Are we now approaching the Great Tribulation and the return of our King?

GLORY: The Future of the Believers
The entire prophetic system explained for those who are going to live it! The Rapture, our time in Heaven, the Kingdom and eternity. Where we go from here. Our rewards, our eternal lives, our entire future.

THE SEVEN FEASTS OF ISRAEL
A complete explanation of the holy days God gave Moses on Mount Sinai, and how each was fulfilled by our Lord. Passover, Pentecost, Trumpets, Tabernacles, etc., fully discussed as to their hidden meanings in the Messiah. A very special section on how every baby in the womb develops according to God's system of the holy days.

STUDY BOOK SERIES *continued*

THE SECOND COMING
The prime difference between the biblical faith and worldly religions is that with the Messiah we have a bright future. What we see is not all we get. The life in this world is of little importance to those who have been promised the Kingdom to come. The return of the King fully explained.

SEVEN CHURCHES: *Does Yours Fit In?*
A refreshing and unusual perspective on the churches presented in Revelation 2 and 3. A Jewish Christian and Bible scholar, Zola looks at these earliest churches from the Old Testament and Jewish traditional point of view. A highly interesting and most useful study, applicable to church life everywhere today.

HOW CAN A GENTILE BE SAVED?
Christians always ask Zola, "How did you come to the Lord?" Their **real** question is, "How can a Jew be saved?" He finally decided to make a biblical inquiry into how they got saved. The results are extremely thought-provoking.

"IN MY FATHER'S HOUSE"
The Lord said, "In my Father's house are many mansions . . . I go to prepare a place for you." An explanation of the incredible seven years we will spend as guests in heaven, in the Messiah's Father's house.

ISRAEL, MY PROMISED
Has God finished with the Jews? Are the modern Israelites the valid Chosen People of the Bible? A sensitive and very personal look at the land of our Lord, as seen today and as promised in the Kingdom.

THE PROMISED LAND
Travel with Zola and the location television crew as they film in the Holy Land. An interesting and entertaining behind-the-scenes look at Israel, with photos and colorful descriptions of sites shown on Zola's weekly programs.